AF316704

Don't Tell A Girl She's Pretty

Written by Nikki Helms

Illustrated by Amurtha Godage

Copyright © 2022. All rights reserved. This book or parts thereof may not be reproduced in any form, stored in any retrieval system, or transmitted in any form by any means—electronic, mechanical, photocopy, recording, or otherwise—without prior written permission of the publisher, except as provided by United States of America copyright law and fair use.

Don't tell a girl she's pretty

When she's good at math and sums.

Tell her she's a problem solver
x2
x4
x8

And watch
what she becomes.

Don't tell a girl she's pretty

When she's also strong and brave.

For "pretty" is no use

If she should see a pup to save.

Don't tell a girl
she's pretty

When she puts a tiara on her head.

She's
the queen
of her
castle

So mention that instead.

Don't tell a
girl she's pretty

Right before
she has a test.

she won't need more distractions

And she'll want to do her best.

Don't tell
a girl she's pretty

And then tell
a boy he's smart.

They BOTH
should be reminded

Of the good
that's in their heart.

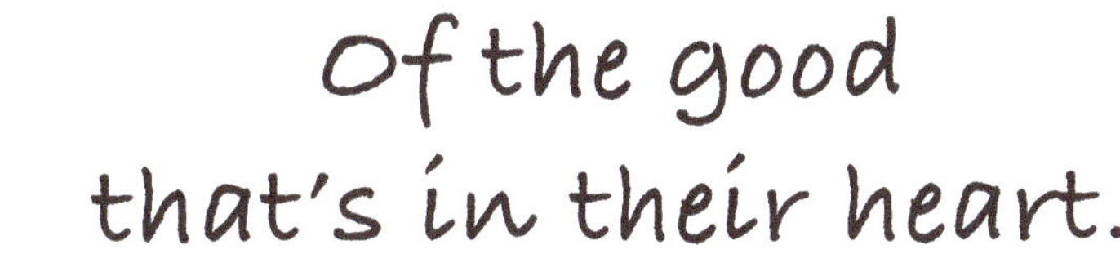

Don't tell the girls they're pretty

While they spin and dance and twirl.

Tell them they're
a graceful group

Of strong
and talented girls.

Don't tell
a girl she's pretty

When she's feeling
down or sad.

There's so much more than "pretty"

In her life to make her glad.

While "pretty" is a lovely word
It's not the only way

To tell a girl how great she is;
Awesome every day!

About The Author

Debut author Nikki Helms, writes to build confidence and social skills in young children. Nikki uses her experiences educating parents, teachers, and leaders on the importance of raising socially responsible unshakable children. She loves dogs, standup comedy, and sewing. Nikki lives in Atlanta, Georgia with her growing family.